Understanding the Elements of the Periodic Table™

SODIUM

Michele Thomas

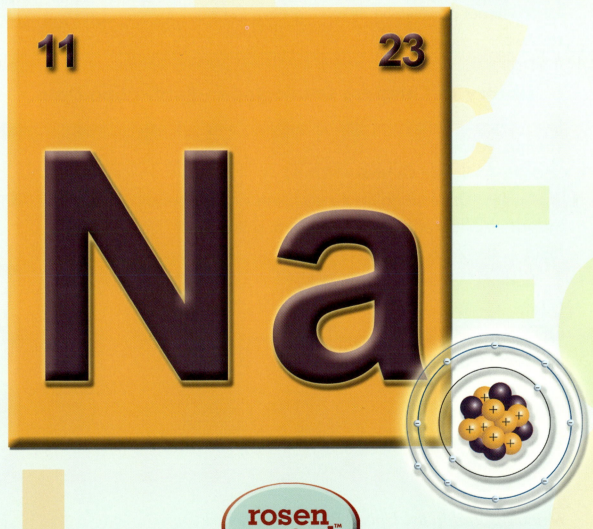

rosen central™

The Rosen Publishing Group, Inc., New York

For my dad, Rufus, salt of the earth, who taught me how to "walk the dog"

Published in 2005 by The Rosen Publishing Group, Inc.
29 East 21st Street, New York, NY 10010

Library of Congress Cataloging-in-Publication Data

Thomas, Michele.
Sodium / Michele Thomas.—1st ed.
   p. cm.—(Understanding the elements of the periodic table)
Includes bibliographical references and index.
ISBN 1-4042-0160-2 (library binding)
1. Sodium—Juvenile literature.
I. Title.
QD181.N2T46 2005
546'.382—dc22

2004009272

On the cover: Sodium's square on the periodic table of elements. Inset: Sodium's atomic structure.

Manufactured in the United States of America

Contents

Introduction

It's easy to think of salt—just sitting there quietly on your dining room table—as the simple stuff of french fries and peanuts at the ballpark. Here, it just looks like a hard, clear crystal that helps to make food taste a little better. However, if we dig a little deeper, we'll see that the story of salt (NaCl, a combination of sodium and chlorine) stretches back thousands of years through Earth's history and human history. Common table salt is just one of the many substances that are made partly of sodium.

According to archaeologists, salt was in general use for thousands of years. Nearly 4,700 years ago, the *Peng-Tzao-Kan-Mu*, one of the earliest known medical books, was written in China. A major portion of this writing was devoted to a discussion of more than forty kinds of salt used for a variety of purposes. One such use was in the treatment of a medical condition called goiter, in which the thyroid gland swells because the body isn't receiving enough iodine (I). Iodine is often found in salt when it is extracted from the earth. According to the *Peng-Tzao-Kan-Mu*, salt was also used to treat infections, to decrease swelling, and as a common headache remedy. Egyptian art from as long ago as 1450 BC shows people trading and using salt for food, money, and mummification.

The ancient Egyptians believed in life after death, and they believed that mummification would guarantee passage into the next

Sodium, in one form or another, has been used by humans for thousands of years. This painting illustrates the embalming process used by ancient Egyptians. The process used salt and other sodium-based substances to help prepare the body for burial. The sodium also helped preserve the body once it was buried.

life. The word "mummy" is derived from the Arabic *mumiyah*, which means "body preserved by wax or bitumen." This term was used because of an Arab misconception of the methods used by the Egyptians in creating mummies. Small packages of natron—a mixture of a powdery, sodium-based mineral and salt—wrapped in linen were placed inside the body. The outside of the body was covered

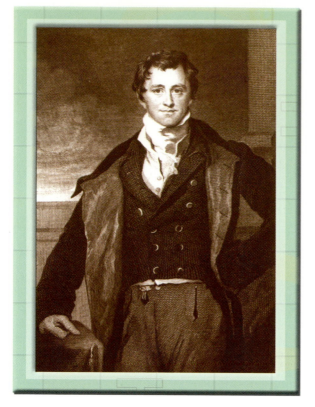

Chemist Sir Humphry Davy is credited with being the first to isolate sodium. Davy followed in the footsteps of other chemists who experimented with electrolysis, a process that uses electricity to separate substances into simple elements. Using electrolysis, Davy was able to isolate sodium.

with loose natron or packages of linen-wrapped natron. The combination of the natron and the hot, dry weather of Egypt worked to remove moisture from the body. Once the body was completely dried out, the packs were removed, and the corpse was given a sponge bath with water. The skin was covered with tree sap, and the body cavity was packed with wads of linen soaked in the same material. The body was then ready to be wrapped in linen strips and bound into the bundle we know as a mummy.

Trade in ancient Greece involving the exchange of salt for slaves gave rise to the expression "not worth his salt," which means that someone or something is not very valuable. Special salt rations given to early Roman soldiers were known as *salarium argentum*, a term which is the root of the English word "salary," which means "payment for work." In fact, the Latin word for salt, *sal*, is also the root word for the modern "sauce" and "sausage," both of which are prepared using salt. In many cultures, offering bread and salt to visitors is considered polite.

Indeed, french fries are only the beginning. The real story of salt—and the element sodium—is quite a salty tale.

Chapter One
What Is Sodium?

Sodium (Na) is an essential element in the diet of both humans and animals, and even of many plants. Salt, perhaps sodium's most common compound, is one of the most effective and most widely used of all food preservatives.

Sodium is the sixth most abundant element on Earth and comprises about 2.8 percent of Earth's crust. Sodium can also be found within the Sun, comets, and the stars, as well as within a thin layer of Earth's atmosphere that begins about 50 miles (80 kilometers) from the planet's surface. Have you ever looked into the night sky? Even on the darkest nights, you can often see a faint light. Scientists believe that it is the presence of sodium in our atmosphere that causes this light. A combination of the Sun's heat and friction at the edge of outer space ignites the tiny amounts of sodium gas in the upper regions of Earth's atmosphere. English chemist Sir Humphry Davy is credited with the discovery of sodium, but German chemist Robert Wilhelm Bunsen actually isolated sodium into its purest form around 1860. Pure sodium can be cut with a knife at room temperature and is brittle at low temperatures.

Davy and the Element

Sir Humphry Davy was on to something. It was the year 1807, and the chemist and professor had been reading up on the work of two other brilliant chemists, Alessandro Volta and William Nicholson. Davy began by researching the work of Volta, an Italian physicist known for his work in the study of electricity and his invention of the first battery in 1800. Davy also studied the work of Nicholson, an English chemist who discovered the electrolysis of water. The electrolysis of water separates water into its basic elements, hydrogen (H) and oxygen (O). During electrolysis, wires are attached to a battery at one end, while the other ends of the wires are placed in a jar of water. When the electric current hits the water, the hydrogen and oxygen in the water will begin to separate and form bubbles at the submerged ends of the wires. Davy

Pictured here are some of the instruments Davy used during his electrochemical experiments in the early nineteenth century. Today, these instruments are housed at the Royal Institution in London, England.

Sodium, the main ingredient in salt, is actually classified as a metal in the periodic table of elements. In its pure form *(pictured)*, sodium is a silvery metal. Unlike most other metal elements, sodium is extremely soft and can easily be cut with a knife. Pure sodium has peculiar characteristics, particularly that it reacts violently with water.

wondered whether electrolysis could be used to separate potash—the ash left over after wood burns—into its basic elements.

To conduct his experiment, Davy built his own electrolysis equipment, consisting of two lead bars, called electrodes, each attached at one end with wire to a battery. After several false starts, small silvery drops formed on one of the electrodes. This metal was like nothing else Davy had seen before. It was soft and extremely lightweight. Davy had succeeded in isolating the basic elements of potash! He called this new metal "potassium," derived from the medieval Latin word *potassa*.

Davy was determined to discover what difference, if any, there was between potash and soda ash, a harsh substance that remained when wood ashes were boiled in water. Davy tried the electrolysis experiment once more using soda ash. The experiment helped to break down the soda ash into hydrogen, oxygen, and another strange silvery metal. It, too, was very soft and lightweight. The metal bubbled and fizzed whenever it came into contact with water, although it floated on the water's surface.

Exposed to air for a long period of time, this new substance started to look a lot like the salt used to flavor food. It even tasted like salt. Davy called this second substance that he discovered "sodium," from the medieval Latin word *sodanum*, meaning "headache remedy," a common use of salt at the time. Little did Davy know, he had discovered one of the essential ingredients for life on Earth—the secret of the ocean, tears, and, yes, salt.

The Element Sodium

Just what is an element anyway? Elements are made of only one kind of substance. They are the building blocks of matter, which you can think of as just about anything and everything that takes up space. Try thinking about matter as a giant puzzle and elements as the puzzle pieces—really, really small puzzle pieces. By fitting one "piece" of sodium (Na) together with one "piece" of chlorine (Cl), you can create a molecule of salt (NaCl). Different combinations of elements create everything in the universe, from plants to planets.

Let's talk a little more about these puzzle pieces and how they fit together. For starters, a more proper name for them would be molecules. If you've ever put together a puzzle of your own, you know that even puzzle pieces must be made of something, like cardboard, plastic, wood, or—in the case of chemistry—atoms. An atom is the smallest piece of an element that can join with another particle to form a molecule. An atom of an element cannot be broken down any further. However, there are even smaller pieces that make up an atom, and these are called subatomic particles.

Subatomic Particles

Atoms themselves are made up of tiny particles called protons, neutrons, and electrons. These are known as subatomic particles. Protons

A sodium atom has eleven protons and twelve neutrons in its nucleus. Eleven electrons orbit, or circle, the nucleus. The one electron in sodium's outermost shell makes this element fairly unstable. A stable atom has an outer shell filled with electrons. Sodium is always on the lookout to lose its outermost electron.

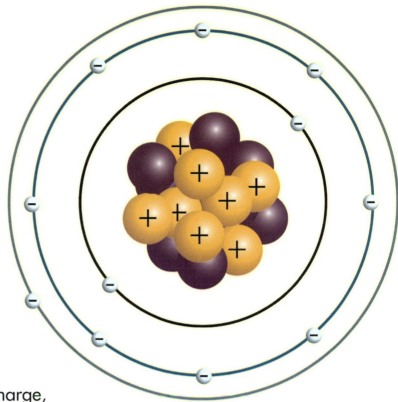

have a positive electric charge, electrons have a negative electric charge, and neutrons have no charge at all.

If you were to view an atom through a very powerful microscope, you would find that it is largely made up of empty space. The rest consists of a positively charged nucleus, which is the center of the atom. Inside the nucleus are protons and neutrons. Surrounding the nucleus are shells of negatively charged electrons. An element's atomic number is the number of protons contained within its nucleus. Sodium has eleven protons in its nucleus. Therefore, its atomic number is 11. Most sodium atoms have twelve neutrons.

The nucleus of a sodium atom is small and heavy compared to the surrounding electrons, which are the lightest charged particles in the universe. If you've ever experimented with magnets, then you probably know that opposites attract—negative and positive charges are drawn toward each other. In an atom, these forces, called electromagnetic forces, bind the electrons to the nucleus and help hold the atoms together.

Sodium Snapshot

Chemical Symbol:	Na
Properties:	Soft, silvery white metal that floats on water and combines easily with many other elements
Discovered By:	Element has been known of since prehistoric times; isolated by English scientist Sir Humphry Davy in 1807
Atomic Number:	11
Atomic Weight:	22.9 amu
Protons:	11
Electrons:	11
Neutrons:	12
Density @ 293 K:	0.971 g/cm^3
Melting Point:	208°F; 97.81°C; 371 K
Boiling Point:	1,621°F; 882.9°C; 1,156.1 K
Commonly Found:	Earth's atmosphere, soil, crust, and oceans, as well as plant and animal life

Outside the nucleus are the shells that contain the electrons. The first shell can hold only two electrons, the second shell can hold up to eight electrons, and the third shell contains up to eighteen. The behavior of an atom is strongly influenced by the electron distribution in shells. The sodium atom has three shells of electrons. The inner shell contains two, the second shell holds eight, and the third is home to only one electron.

Pure Sodium: Naturally Unstable

So, how does the number of electrons impact the behavior of a sodium atom? The more room an atom has in its electron shells, the more unstable it is, meaning how readily it combines with other elements to form different substances. An atom is the most stable when its electron shells are completely full. In that case, there's no more room in the electron shell, and the element has no need to borrow or share electrons.

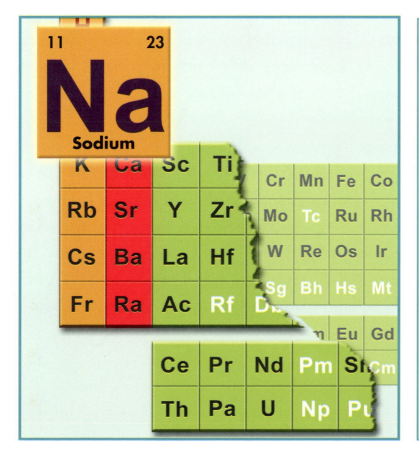

Sodium is represented by the letters Na, short for the Egyptian word *natron*, which was a substance used in their mummification process. The number in the upper-left corner represents the element's atomic number, which is the number of protons in one atom of the element. The number in the upper-right corner represents atomic weight, which is the average sum of protons and neutrons in one atom of the element.

Just a little bit of sodium will react violently with water. After a small piece of pure sodium is dropped in a jar of water, the sodium reacts. The sodium sparks and seems to ignite while it dances around the water. The water then begins to bubble *(photo 1)*. Eventually, the reaction gets so intense the sodium explodes *(photo 2)*.

Knowing that sodium has an atomic number of 11, we also know that it has eleven protons and eleven electrons. With only one electron in its outer shell, sodium is always on the lookout for other elements to give away that single electron. This means that sodium is very reactive and combines easily with many substances. After donating its outermost electron, the sodium atom's second shell (which is full) becomes the outer shell. The atom then becomes stable.

In fact, sodium is one of the most reactive elements in the universe. Pure sodium is never found in nature. It can only be extracted by using electrolysis, which breaks apart sodium's bond with other substances. Once isolated, pure sodium must be kept in a nonreactive, or inert, environment, such as in nitrogen (N) or in liquids such as kerosene or naphtha. In water, sodium will appear to fizz as it reacts with the oxygen in the water to form sodium oxide, releasing pure hydrogen gas.

Chapter Two
Sodium and the Periodic Table

Scientists have discovered more than 100 elements so far. As old as Earth is (nearly 4.5 billion years old), many of these discoveries were made during the last few hundred years. As we've seen, sodium, for example, was only discovered by Sir Humphry Davy at the start of the nineteenth century.

With so many discoveries to keep track of, scientists soon began to look for ways to organize the elements they had found. In 1869, a Russian chemist and professor at the University of St. Petersburg, Dmitry Mendeleyev, created a special table to help his students remember the elements. He assigned symbols to each element and placed them in horizontal rows, or periods, according to their atomic weight, with the lightest in each row at the left and the heaviest at the right. Sodium has been assigned the chemical symbol Na, from the word "natron," the salt mixture used to prepare mummies in ancient Egypt.

Little did Mendeleyev know, his arrangement was a simple idea that would help revolutionize the way scientists understood chemistry. The table allowed scientists to really see for the first time the relationships, trends, and patterns among elements. Mendeleyev's table had gaps, but he predicted that these gaps would soon be filled by elements not yet discovered. He also guessed that these new elements would have properties that could be predicted based on their placement in what he

In the late 1800s, the work of Russian chemist Dmitry Mendeleyev was groundbreaking, and it is still used today. Mendeleyev is credited with designing and publishing the very first periodic table of elements. He designed the table to help his students understand the relationship between the elements. Mendeleyev claimed that the final solution for the table came to him in a dream.

called the periodic table of the elements. He was quite right, as it turns out. Within twenty years after he first created the periodic table, three new elements would be discovered, and they each possessed the properties that Mendeleyev had predicted.

Although the table was not widely accepted at first, scientists eventually realized that it was a pretty good idea. In fact, the modern periodic table is very similar to Mendeleyev's original design. Today, the periodic table is arranged in horizontal rows called periods. In each period, the elements are arranged in the order of their atomic numbers.

The elements are also organized into eighteen vertical groups numbered IA through VIIA, IB through VIIIB, and 0. The number of the group appears above each column of the table. In the same way that members of a family often resemble one another, elements within these groups also have similar chemical properties. In fact, they are often referred to as families of elements. By arranging the elements this way, scientists could predict whether any given element was a metal, a nonmetal, or a metalloid, which is an element that has the properties of both a metal and a nonmetal.

Two New Elements

When Mendeleyev published his idea for the periodic table in 1869, he left gaps in the table's design. This would allow for new elements to be added as they were discovered. Since Mendeleyev published his work, more than fifty elements have been added to the table. This trend has continued into the twenty-first century. Recently, a team of American and Russian scientists created two new elements with atomic numbers 113 and 115. Element 113 is named ununtrium (Uut); element 115 is named ununpentium (Uup). However, the existence of Uut and Uup is still in question. Before new elements can be added to the periodic table, they have to be verified by other scientists.

Sodium Takes a Place at the Table

Now, let's take a closer look at the periodic table. Sodium is located within group IA on the periodic table, which also contains lithium (Li), potassium (K), rubidium (Rb), cesium (Cs), and francium (Fr). These elements are known as the alkali metals. Alkali metals are very reactive metals that do not occur freely in their pure form. These metals each have only one electron in their outer shell, and they very often give it away or share it with other elements in an effort to become more stable. The elements within group IA behave more similarly to each other than elements in any other group of the periodic table. As you move down the group from lithium to francium, each element reacts more easily with other elements. In other words, the elements grow more reactive. As you can see, hydrogen is often placed in group IA on the table because it, too, has only one electron in its outer shell. However, it isn't an alkali metal but a gas.

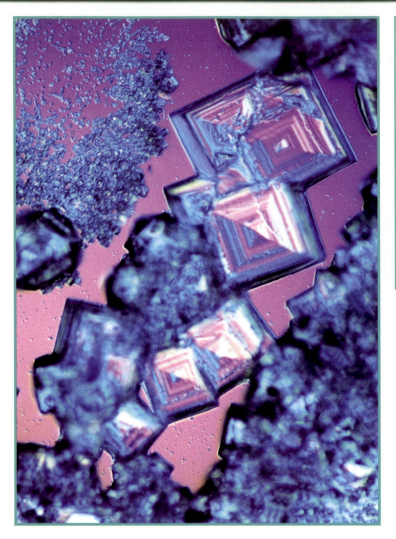

Common table salt (NaCl) is composed of thousands of tiny crystals. This photo captures salt crystals in a cubic lattice structure. These crystals are formed by the joining of a positively charged sodium ion with a negatively charged chlorine ion. These ions join together in repeating units to create a crystal.

Properties of Sodium

Properties are the characteristics of an element. They are what make the element unique. For example, your eyes, nose, and hair color are properties that help tell you apart from other members of your family.

Each of the group IA elements, including sodium, are silver metals. They are soft and can be easily cut with a knife to expose a shiny surface that becomes dull when exposed to air. As with all metals, the alkali metals are good conductors of heat and electricity.

All elements on the periodic table can appear in one of three physical states or phases: solid, liquid, or gas. Sodium is a solid at room temperature. However, when heated to 208°F (97.81°C), it melts into a thick liquid. If you continue to heat it, sodium will boil into a gas at 1,621°F (882.9°C).

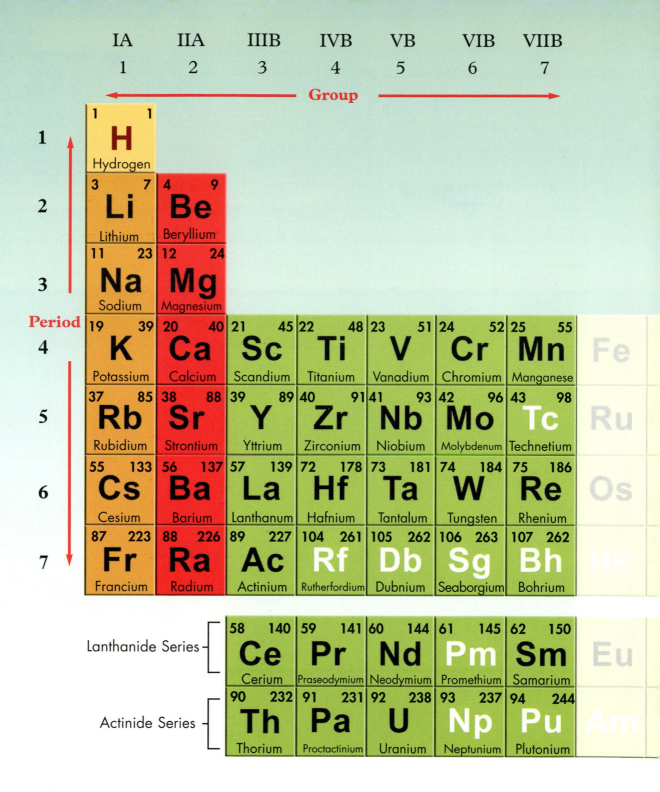

	IA 1	IIA 2	IIIB 3	IVB 4	VB 5	VIB 6	VIIB 7	
1	1 1 **H** Hydrogen							
2	3 7 **Li** Lithium	4 9 **Be** Beryllium						
3	11 23 **Na** Sodium	12 24 **Mg** Magnesium						
4	19 39 **K** Potassium	20 40 **Ca** Calcium	21 45 **Sc** Scandium	22 48 **Ti** Titanium	23 51 **V** Vanadium	24 52 **Cr** Chromium	25 55 **Mn** Manganese	Fe
5	37 85 **Rb** Rubidium	38 88 **Sr** Strontium	39 89 **Y** Yttrium	40 91 **Zr** Zirconium	41 93 **Nb** Niobium	42 96 **Mo** Molybdenum	43 98 **Tc** Technetium	Ru
6	55 133 **Cs** Cesium	56 137 **Ba** Barium	57 139 **La** Lanthanum	72 178 **Hf** Hafnium	73 181 **Ta** Tantalum	74 184 **W** Tungsten	75 186 **Re** Rhenium	Os
7	87 223 **Fr** Francium	88 226 **Ra** Radium	89 227 **Ac** Actinium	104 261 **Rf** Rutherfordium	105 262 **Db** Dubnium	106 263 **Sg** Seaborgium	107 262 **Bh** Bohrium	Hs

Group

Period

Lanthanide Series

58 140 **Ce** Cerium	59 141 **Pr** Praseodymium	60 144 **Nd** Neodymium	61 145 **Pm** Promethium	62 150 **Sm** Samarium	Eu

Actinide Series

90 232 **Th** Thorium	91 231 **Pa** Proctactinium	92 238 **U** Uranium	93 237 **Np** Neptunium	94 244 **Pu** Plutonium	Am

Sodium sits in group IA of the periodic table, the very far left vertical row. This group is known as the hydrogen group and includes the alkali metals lithium (Li), potassium (K), rubidium (Rb), cesium (Cs), and francium (Fr). These elements in group IA all react violently with water and release hydrogen as a result.

Sodium Isotopes

A small number of sodium atoms have extra neutrons. These are called isotopes. You might think of an element as a family and isotopes as family members. Isotopes have the same atomic number, but they often have slightly different physical properties. Sodium 24, a sodium isotope, contains eleven protons and thirteen neutrons. It is slightly radioactive, which means that it naturally releases a certain kind of energy. Most chemical elements have one or more isotopes. Because they have no electrical charge, the presence of extra neutrons usually has little to no effect on the properties of the element. However, the neutrons can change the substance's atomic weight (or atomic mass). Sodium has an atomic weight of 22.9. The atomic weight is the average sum of the number of protons and neutrons in each atom of the element. Electrons are very light and do not really contribute much to the atomic weight.

Chapter Three
Salts and the Seas

If you've ever accidentally swallowed seawater while swimming in the ocean, then you no doubt have noticed that it is very, very salty. Sodium makes up about 1.05 percent of Earth's oceans and seas.

So how did the sea become so salty? To answer this question, we first have to take a closer look at sodium ions. When a sodium atom reacts with another element, it gives up the single electron in its outer shell. When this occurs, there are no longer eleven electrons to balance the eleven protons that are in the nucleus of a sodium atom. The sodium atom then becomes a positively charged sodium ion, written as $Na+$. Within the earth's crust, sodium ions often combine with the oxygen in soil and rocks to form sodium oxide (Na_2O), one of the most common forms of sodium found in the earth's crust. As it rains, the water runs over the earth's crust and down into rivers, picking up sodium oxide, chlorine, and other minerals along the way. As the water moves, the substances in the water, like the sodium oxide and chlorine, combine as they come into contact with each other. For instance, in water, sodium ions combine with chlorine ions to form sodium chloride. As water flows in rivers, it picks up small amounts of mineral salts from the rocks and soil of the riverbeds. This salty water flows into the oceans and seas. As the ocean water slowly evaporates from sunlight or freezes under polar ice, the salt remains dissolved in the ocean—it

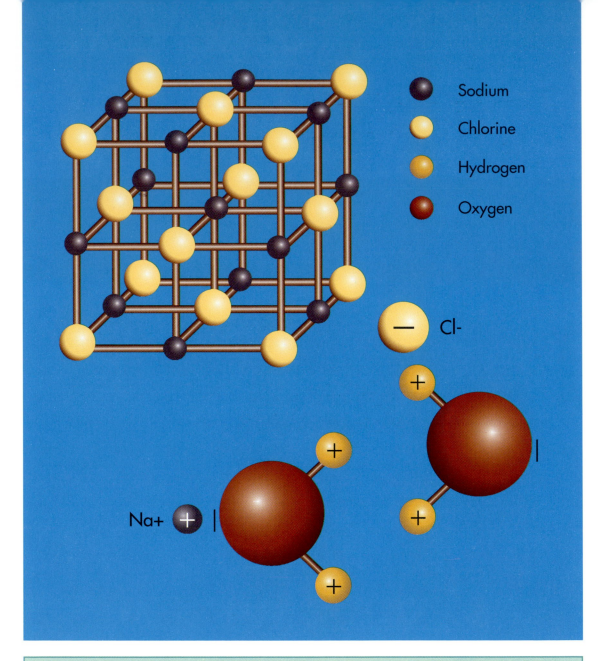

The molecular structure of seawater includes sodium, chlorine, hydrogen, and oxygen. The positively charged sodium ion is attracted to the negatively charged side of the water molecule. The negatively charged chlorine ion is attracted to the positively charged side of the water molecule. The combination creates a complex structure of bonds *(upper left)* to create molecules of seawater.

does not evaporate. As a result, the remaining water gets saltier and saltier as time passes.

Nearly two-thirds of the solid material dissolved in the sea is sodium chloride. However, the amount of salt in seawater can vary at different places and times. For example, in the Arctic, there are huge icebergs, which float along the Arctic Ocean like giant ice cubes. As they melt, they release freshwater into the ocean. This dilutes the salt content of the sea in the Arctic.

Chemical Salts

The common salt found on french fries and peanuts is really only one kind of salt used today. In chemistry, a salt is a type of compound created when a substance called a base, or alkaline substance, is neutralized by another substance called an acid. When an acid is neutralized, the number of electrons or ions that it has is completely balanced by those of another substance, so it does not continue to react chemically with its environment. Acids are substances that form hydrogen ions when dissolved in water. They usually have a bit of a sour taste, like grapefruit or lemon juice, for example. Alkalis easily accept the hydrogen ions created by an acid. They also usually have a bitter taste.

Harvesting Salt

A large amount of the salt that eventually shows up on your dining room table is found naturally in deposits around the world. Some of these are thousands of feet thick, while still others are the remains of ancient salt lakes like Utah's Great Salt Lake and the Dead Sea in Israel. In the United States, nearly 85 percent of what becomes table salt is mined from deep within the earth, where salt deposits formed as ancient lakes and oceans evaporated over millions of years. Some layers of salt are found so far beneath the earth's surface that they cannot be reached with mining equipment. In other places around the world, water from rain or the runoff from rivers and lakes has penetrated salt deposits but has not been able to evaporate, thus forming an underground

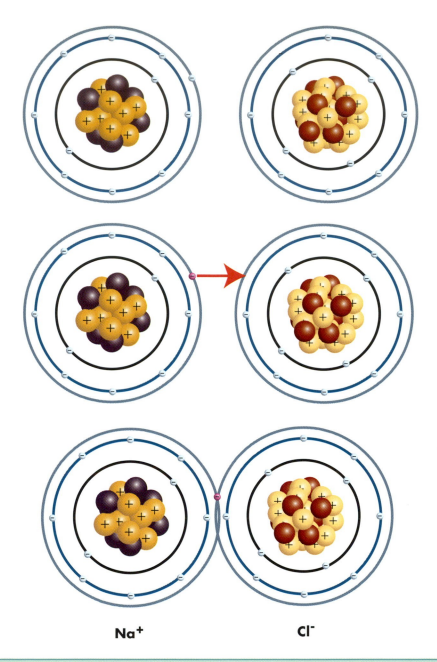

Na⁺   Cl⁻

Sodium chloride is formed by an electrostatic bond. When one sodium ion meets one chlorine ion, the sodium ion is ready to donate its one outermost electron *(middle)*. After the sodium ion donates its electron, a very strong bond is formed between the two ions *(bottom)*. Together, the sodium and chlorine ions create a stable molecule of sodium chloride.

brine (salty water) well. Thick and sludgy, brine is the substance that Alessandro Volta used to wet the cloth he used in the construction of the voltaic pile, a series of several metal discs each separated by a damp cloth to create a continuous current. The brine from a brine well can be pumped up to the surface of the ground, where the water in the brine evaporates, leaving salt crystals behind.

In a similar process, salt water from the ocean is pumped into large ponds, where it is allowed to evaporate, leaving salt crystals on the bottom of the pond. As the seawater evaporates, different chemicals in the water crystallize into minerals at different times. In this way, scientists and industry workers can mine salts of bromine (Br), a gas, and magnesium (Mg), a metal, as well as sodium chloride.

Sodium and Soil

Have you ever noticed a white crusty substance around the shore of a lake or ocean? This white crust is a mixture of minerals, including

Salt of the Earth

When freshwater is pumped to the earth's surface, it is coming from an aquifer, a special kind of rocky area within the earth. When you dig a well, you are also digging into an aquifer. In recent years, more water has been removed from aquifers than has been naturally replaced by water seeping into the ground from rain. Some aquifers near the ocean allow salt water to seep in, and when water is pumped from these locations, it is a good deal saltier than normal. In fact, some experts believe that this is the reason why the drinking water going to millions of homes around the world contains more salt than ever. When this saltier freshwater is used to water crops, lawns, and gardens, the soil becomes saltier as well. Over time, the soil may build up so much salt that it becomes difficult to grow any plants at all. To remedy this, scientists and farmers are working together to find ways to remove the salt from the water before it is used on crops.

Sodium chloride, or salt, can build up along shorelines of salty bodies of water. Here, salt deposits line the shore of the Great Salt Lake in Utah. The Great Salt Lake, North America's largest inland body of salt water, has a much greater level of salinity than seawater. This means that there is more dissolved salt per unit of water in the Great Salt Lake.

sodium chloride, that crystallized when the Sun's heat evaporated the water nearest to the shore.

Most water, including rainwater, contains some salts, which can build up in soil. For the most part, these salts come from river water that has washed over the riverbanks or from the weathering of nearby rocks. This is, in part, how sodium became the sixth most common element in the earth's surface. As mentioned, salt also builds up in the soil when farmers irrigate their crops with water that contains too much salt. If such water is used very often, it can make the soil too salty for growing plants in.

Chapter Four
Sodium and Our World

Sodium, in the form of salt, is extremely important to food preservation. Salt is one of the world's oldest methods of preserving food. To understand why, we first have to understand salt's unique relationship with moisture. Food becomes unsafe to eat because tiny life-forms like bacteria and mold, which can harm people, come into contact with the food. However, most of these microorganisms can only live in a moist environment and cannot exist in food if there is no moisture present. This is where salt comes in. Salt preserves food by drying out the bacteria and mold, thus preventing the food from spoilage.

The term "osmosis" describes the process by which a solvent (or liquid substance) moves from an area that contains more solvent to an area where there is less solvent. Osmosis occurs when this moisture moves through the thin outer wall, or membrane, of a plant or animal cell. Salt draws water out of the bacteria, taking away the moisture that bacteria need to survive. Osmosis is a natural process and would occur without salt. However, it would happen much more slowly, allowing more time for bacteria to attack and spoil food.

Soaps

Sodium is also an important part of soap. In any body of water, each water molecule is surrounded and attracted to other water molecules.

Salt can preserve food or make it taste delicious by bringing out its natural flavor. Here, salt is shoveled onto a pile of hams. Salt can also preserve food by decreasing the amount of water molecules in the food. Bacteria, which spoil food, cannot grow in foods that contain salt.

However, at the surface of water, the water molecules are surrounded by other water molecules only on one side. On the other side, air molecules touch the water molecules, creating tension on the surface of the water. This surface tension causes water to bead up on surfaces like glass or fabric, which slows the cleaning process by slowing down how long it takes something to become wet. You can see surface tension at work by placing a drop of water on a countertop. The drop will hold its shape and will not spread.

In order for soap to clean, surface tension must be reduced so water can spread and wet surfaces. Chemicals that are able to do this effectively are called surface-active agents, or surfactants. They are said to make water "wetter." Surfactants perform other important functions in cleaning, such as loosening, emulsifying (dispersing in water), and trapping the soil outside of the substance until it can be rinsed away. Soap, detergent, and other chemicals used in cleaning are surfactants.

Soaps are sodium or potassium salts of fatty acids that dissolve in water. They are made by treating fatty acids chemically with a strong chemical salt of an alkali metal such as sodium or potassium that dissolves in water. Fatty acids are weak acids composed of two parts: a carboxylic acid group molecule consisting of one carbon atom, two oxygen atoms, and one hydrogen atom, plus a hydrocarbon chain attached to the carboxylic acid group. Generally, they are made up of a long straight chain of carbon atoms each carrying two hydrogen atoms.

Many years ago, the alkalis used in making soap were obtained from the ashes of burned wood and were mixed with oil and fat. However, during the late eighteenth century, a French chemist named Nicolas Leblanc developed a way to produce sodium hydroxide (NaOH) and sodium carbonate (Na_2CO_3) out of table salt. Sodium hydroxide would become the most important ingredient in effective soap. During the Leblanc process, table salt was first converted into a compound called sodium sulfate (Na_2SO_4) by mixing it with sulfuric acid. The sodium sulfate was then roasted with chalk or limestone ($CaCO_3$) and coal to produce a mixture of sodium carbonate and sulfur. The carbonate was filtered out with water, and the solution crystallized. The Leblanc process was adopted throughout Europe within just a few years. However, over the past century, many soap-making processes have come and gone with each process rendering the previous one obsolete.

How Soaps Are Made

There are two major ways to make soap. Saponification of fats and oils is the most widely used soap-making process. This method involves heating fats and oils and combining them with a liquid alkali, such as sodium hydroxide, to produce soap, water, and an oily substance called glycerol. Many years ago, women used the glycerol that was produced during soap making as a moisturizing lotion for their skin. The other major soap-making process is the neutralization of fatty acids with an alkali. Fats and oils are split by using high-pressure steam to yield fatty acids and glycerin. The fatty acids are mixed with and neutralized by an alkali to produce soap and water. When the alkali is sodium hydroxide, a sodium soap is formed.

How Soaps Work

Soap is great for cleaning because of its ability to act as an emulsifying agent. An emulsifier is a chemical that can suspend oil and dirt in such a way that they can be removed with water. Each soap molecule has a long hydrocarbon chain, sometimes called its "tail," with a carboxylic "head." The head of a soap molecule is made up of a positively charged sodium ion attached to a negatively charged carboxylic ion. The head is called the hydrophilic (water-loving) end. It does not mix easily with oily substances and breaks apart easily in water. The tail of the molecule is called the hydrophobic (water-fearing) end. This end does not dissolve in water and bonds easily with oily or greasy substances, which are the biggest troublemakers when it comes to getting the laundry clean. During the washing process, the hydrophilic end of the soap molecule decreases the surface tension of the water so that the water can be easily absorbed into the cloth. In other words, it makes it easier to wet the cloth. The hydrophobic end of the soap molecule helps pull dirt molecules out of the cloth by chemically bonding with them. Clusters of soap molecules, called micelles, form with their "water-loving" ends facing outward. Each micelle forms around a tiny particle of dirt, trapping it away from the

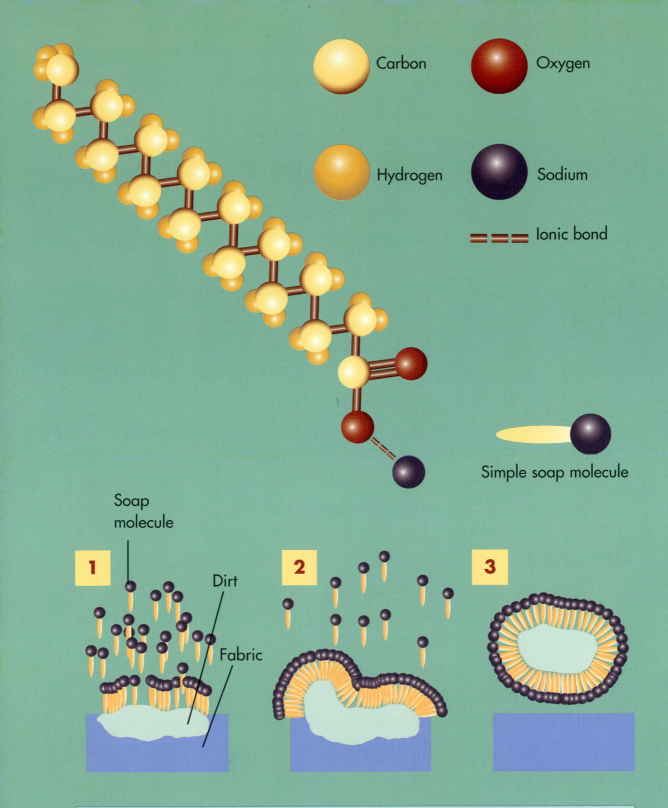

Carbon

Hydrogen

Oxygen

Sodium

Ionic bond

Simple soap molecule

Soap
molecule

Dirt

Fabric

1

2

3

Ever wonder how soap works? It's simple. The soap molecule has a tail that is hydrophobic, meaning it repels water. When soap and water are added to a dirty surface, the soap molecules attack the dirt. The hydrophobic tails of the soap molecules then push apart the hydrogen molecules located in the water *(model 1)*. Then the soap molecules work their way in between the dirt and the fabric *(model 2)*. Finally, the soap molecules surround the dirt and hold it away from the fabric where it can be washed away with water *(model 3)*.

clothing until the force of flowing water washes away both the dirt and the soap.

The Many Uses of Sodium Hydroxide

Sodium hydroxide, also called caustic soda or lye, is a very dangerous chemical; just one drop can burn your skin. However, it's also a very important chemical with many uses beyond making soap. Its ability to corrode, or eat away at, other substances makes it the main ingredient in drain cleaners.

Did you ever wonder how paper is made out of trees? Sodium hydroxide plays an important role in making paper. Cellulose, a fibrous plant material, is the basic material used to make most papers. The cellulose of soft woods, like birch and pine, must be dissolved and softened before it can be made into something called wood pulp, which is used to make paper. Cellulose can be a pretty tough material and won't dissolve in water or alcohol, but a solution of sodium hydroxide is just strong enough to do the trick. It makes the cellulose fibers swell so that they are softer and easier to work with during the paper-making process.

Cellophane, the film often used to make packaging and clear tape, is also made from cellulose. In this case, the wood pulp is first treated with several chemicals to turn it into a thick fluid called viscose. The viscose is then pressed out into thin layers and treated with another sodium chemical called sodium sulfate (Na_2SO_4). Then it goes through another complex set of steps to become the clear film used to wrap packages.

Olives are also treated with a sodium hydroxide solution before they are bottled or canned. By neutralizing a chemical called a glucoside, which makes the olives taste bitter, the sodium hydroxide solution helps make the olives taste better.

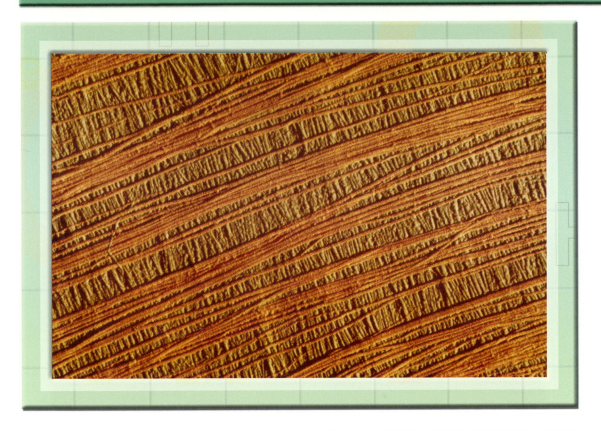

Sodium hydroxide is an important ingredient in papermaking. Cellulose fibers, pictured here under a microscope, are softened and dissolved by sodium hydroxide. The substance is then turned into a pulp matter, which is used to create paper.

Sodium and Fireworks

Creating firework colors is a difficult job that combines art and science. The points of light ejected from fireworks (called stars) require an oxygen-producing chemical to sustain burning, a fuel, a color producer, and a substance called a binder to keep everything where it needs to be. There are two main mechanisms of color production in fireworks: incandescence and luminescence. Incandescence is light produced from heat. Heat causes a substance to become hot and glow, giving off red, orange, yellow, and white light as it becomes hotter. When the temperature of a firework is controlled, the glow of components can be

Sodium plays an important part in giving fireworks their bright shining lights. When burned, different elements can produce different colors of light. Sodium used in fireworks can produce a gold or yellow light.

manipulated to be the desired color at the proper time. Sodium is used in fireworks to give them a gold or yellow color.

Luminescence is light produced by energy sources other than heat. Sometimes luminescence is called "cold light" because it can

The Chemistry of Firework Colors

These elements are used to produce different colors in fireworks.

	Element
red	strontium (Sr), lithium (Li)
orange	calcium (Ca)
gold	iron (Fe), sodium (Na)
yellow	sodium
white	magnesium (Mg), aluminum (Al)
green	barium (Ba) mixed with chlorine (Cl)
blue	copper (Cu) mixed with chlorine
purple	strontium mixed with copper
silver	aluminum, titanium (Ti), or magnesium

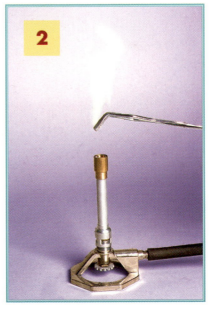

Sodium produces a colored light when burned. Here, a piece of pure sodium is placed over a Bunsen burner *(left)*. After a few moments, the sodium ignites and produces a yellowish flame *(right)*.

occur at or below room temperature. To produce luminescence, energy is absorbed by an electron of an atom or molecule, causing it to become excited and move quickly. When the electron returns to a lower energy state, excess energy is released in the form of a light. The amount of energy present determines the color. Pure colors require pure ingredients. Even tiny amounts of sodium can affect the way a "star" appears.

Sodium on the Street

Sodium-vapor lamps, electric lamps containing a small amount of sodium and neon gas, are used in generating light for streets and highways. These sodium-vapor lamps work when an electric charge jumps between two electrodes, igniting the sodium gas, which gives off a yellow light.

About 0.15 percent of the human body by weight consists of sodium, mostly in the form of sodium chloride. Other elements needed in large amounts by the human body are oxygen (65 percent), carbon (18 percent), hydrogen (10 percent), nitrogen (3 percent), calcium (1.5 percent), phosphorus (1 percent), potassium (0.35 percent), sulfur (0.25 percent), sodium (0.155 percent), chlorine (0.15 percent), magnesium (0.05 percent), iron (0.0004 percent), and iodine (0.00004 percent). Sodium is the most common element found in the blood and body fluids, and it plays a major role in regulating the amount of water throughout the body. Its passage in and out of cells through pores called ion channels is essential for many body functions, including sending electrical signals in the brain and muscles.

Electrolytes

Table salt is formed by ionic bonds between sodium and chlorine. When salt is dissolved in water, the bonds break, releasing positively charged sodium ions and negatively charged chlorine ions into the water. This liquid will conduct electricity. Fluids and ions within the human body that perform this way are called electrolytes. Sodium, calcium, potassium, and magnesium all work in the human body as electrolytes.

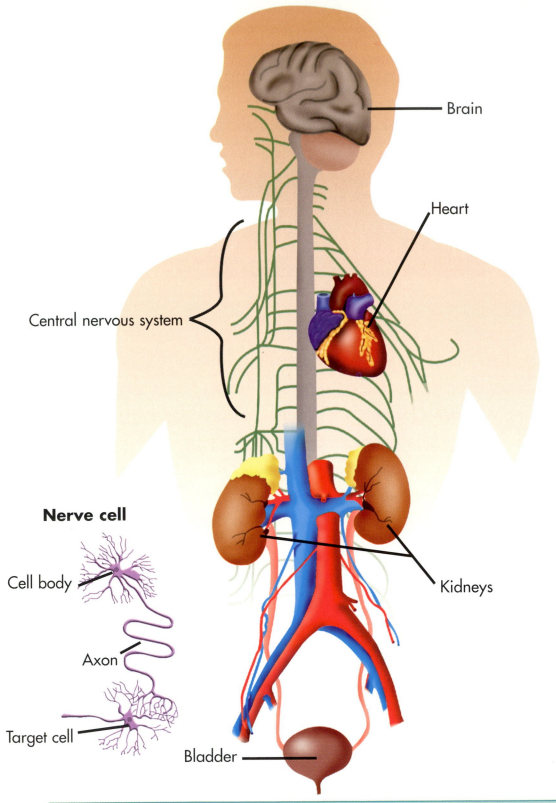

Brain

Heart

Central nervous system

Nerve cell

Cell body

Axon

Target cell

Kidneys

Bladder

Electrolytes are what your cells use to carry electrical impulses, such as nerve impulses. Electrolytes work in the nerve cell *(lower left)* by sending messages to the target cell (located in a muscle). Kidneys hold the electrolyte concentrations in your body. When you sweat, you release sodium and potassium electrolytes.

Electrolytes in the blood help the body function properly. For example, they play an important role in movement. In the nervous system, they send tiny electrical signals to nerve cells. When the nerve cells receive this signal, they release a chemical called acetylcholine, which travels to a nearby muscle fiber and prepares it to accept the sodium and potassium ions coming its way. As they travel, these ions signal other calcium ions to help set up a series of chemical reactions that cause your muscles to move.

Water continually circulates through the body, especially in plasma, the liquid part of the blood. A large part of this flow happens because of the concentration of sodium chloride.

Within the body, sodium ions are needed in high concentrations outside of cells and in low concentrations within cells. As blood moves through the organs of the body, substances move in and out of the blood by osmosis. For example, whenever you drink a glass of water, far more of that water passes through your kidneys than is released as urine. As the blood carries waste products from the body into the kidneys, water flows through the kidneys and back into the blood through osmosis. As this happens, the waste substances gather in one place to exit from your body as urine. Some salt and water are always eliminated along with the waste, which is why it's important that your diet includes salt (in moderation) and water to replenish what is lost.

Sodium Bicarbonate

In the 1860s, Belgian chemist Ernest Solvay discovered a way to make sodium bicarbonate ($NaHCO_3$), the amazing chemical we call baking soda. First, Solvay heated calcium carbonate, or limestone—a light-colored rock often used in building. When heated or burned, limestone breaks down into calcium oxide (CaO), also known as lime, and carbon dioxide (CO_2). The carbon dioxide was mixed with a solution of

Belgian chemist Ernest Solvay was the first to discover a way to make sodium bicarbonate. Today, his creation can be found in many everyday items, including baking soda, certain cleaning products, fire extinguishers, and antacids.

sodium chloride and ammonia (NH_3) to produce sodium bicarbonate and ammonium chloride (NH_4Cl).

Sodium bicarbonate has a truly astonishing number of uses. When mixed with flour and water to make dough, baking soda becomes carbon dioxide. As this happens, bubbles are formed in the dough that make it lighter. This process gives bread, biscuits, and other baked foods their fluffy texture.

Baking soda is useful in treating heartburn, a painful condition that occurs when the stomach produces too much acid. The baking soda neutralizes the acid but often produces carbon dioxide gas as a side effect. This gas can cause pressure on the stomach, making a person feel very uncomfortable.

Have you ever noticed that many toothpastes on the market today contain baking soda? This is because baking soda is also a gentle abrasive that can make teeth whiter, while naturally absorbing odors. This odor-absorbing quality is also the reason why many people keep a box of baking soda in the refrigerator and in the closet, near smelly shoes.

Baking soda acts as a cleaning agent because it is a mild base that can cause dirt and grease to dissolve easily in water for effective removal. Because it is gentle, baking soda can be used to clean glass, chrome, steel,

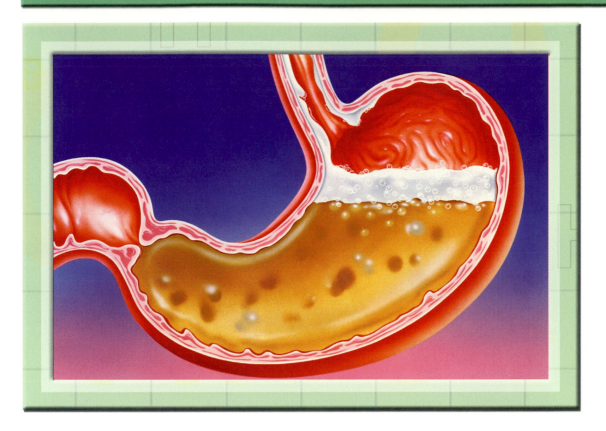

Heartburn *(illustrated above)* is a terrible ailment that affects millions of Americans. It occurs when the acids located in the stomach flow back into the esophagus and the throat. The result causes serious discomfort. Antacids, which contain sodium bicarbonate, neutralize the acid and can cure heartburn.

sinks, tubs, tile, microwaves, and plastic without harm. Industrially, baking soda is used to clean machinery and commercial kitchen equipment.

Sodium bicarbonate is also the main ingredient in a certain type of powdered fire extinguisher used to fight electrical fires. When sprayed onto a fire, the heat of the fire breaks down the chemical into water, a salt, and carbon dioxide. The carbon dioxide cuts off the supply of oxygen to the flames so that they quickly die out.

Throughout this book, we have seen how one little element affects the world around us. Sodium makes our food tasty, keeps our oceans salty, and helps clean our clothes. Most important, sodium keeps us healthy by helping our bodies function properly. We couldn't live without sodium!

The Periodic Table of Elements

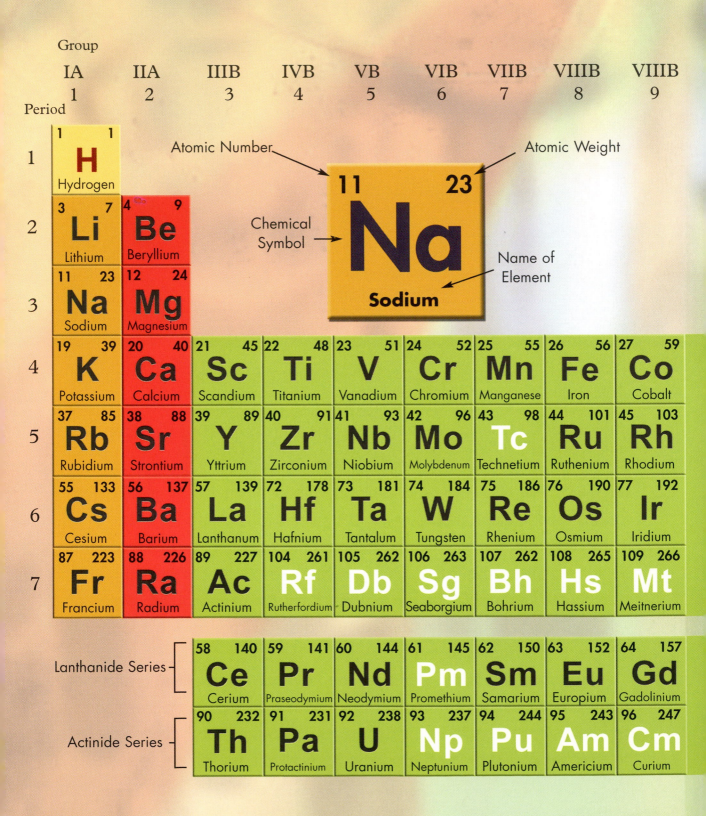

Group

| IA | IIA | IIIB | IVB | VB | VIB | VIIB | VIIIB | VIIIB |
| 1 | 2 | 3 | 4 | 5 | 6 | 7 | 8 | 9 |

Period

Atomic Number

Atomic Weight

Chemical Symbol

11   23
Na
Sodium

Name of Element

1

| 1 1 |
| **H** |
| Hydrogen |

2

3 7	4 9
Li	**Be**
Lithium	Beryllium

3

11 23	12 24
Na	**Mg**
Sodium	Magnesium

4

19 39	20 40	21 45	22 48	23 51	24 52	25 55	26 56	27 59
K	**Ca**	**Sc**	**Ti**	**V**	**Cr**	**Mn**	**Fe**	**Co**
Potassium	Calcium	Scandium	Titanium	Vanadium	Chromium	Manganese	Iron	Cobalt

5

37 85	38 88	39 89	40 91	41 93	42 96	43 98	44 101	45 103
Rb	**Sr**	**Y**	**Zr**	**Nb**	**Mo**	**Tc**	**Ru**	**Rh**
Rubidium	Strontium	Yttrium	Zirconium	Niobium	Molybdenum	Technetium	Ruthenium	Rhodium

6

55 133	56 137	57 139	72 178	73 181	74 184	75 186	76 190	77 192
Cs	**Ba**	**La**	**Hf**	**Ta**	**W**	**Re**	**Os**	**Ir**
Cesium	Barium	Lanthanum	Hafnium	Tantalum	Tungsten	Rhenium	Osmium	Iridium

7

87 223	88 226	89 227	104 261	105 262	106 263	107 262	108 265	109 266
Fr	**Ra**	**Ac**	**Rf**	**Db**	**Sg**	**Bh**	**Hs**	**Mt**
Francium	Radium	Actinium	Rutherfordium	Dubnium	Seaborgium	Bohrium	Hassium	Meitnerium

Lanthanide Series

58 140	59 141	60 144	61 145	62 150	63 152	64 157
Ce	**Pr**	**Nd**	**Pm**	**Sm**	**Eu**	**Gd**
Cerium	Praseodymium	Neodymium	Promethium	Samarium	Europium	Gadolinium

Actinide Series

90 232	91 231	92 238	93 237	94 244	95 243	96 247
Th	**Pa**	**U**	**Np**	**Pu**	**Am**	**Cm**
Thorium	Protactinium	Uranium	Neptunium	Plutonium	Americium	Curium

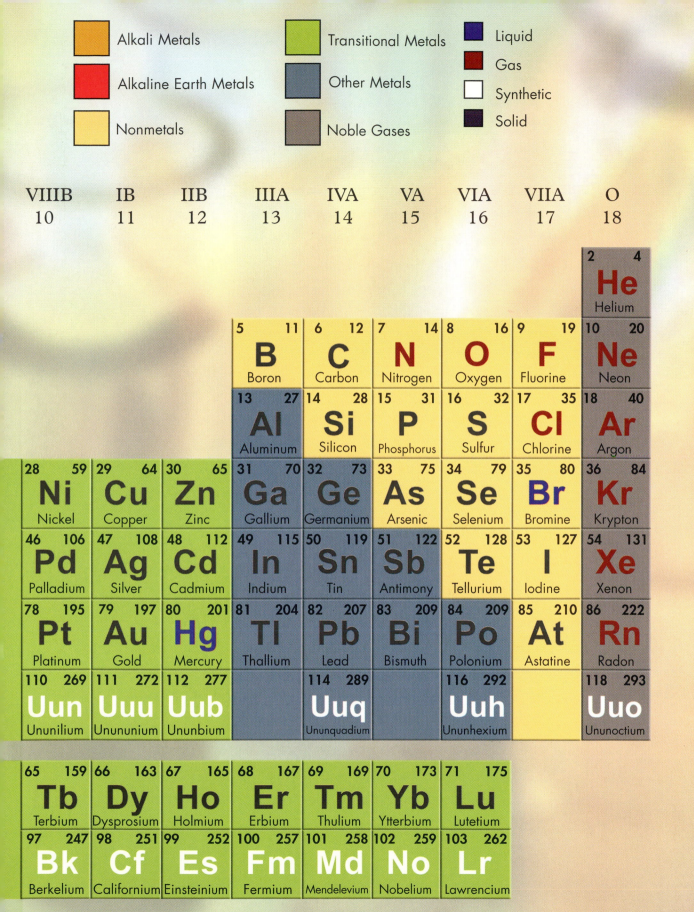

Glossary

acid A reactive substance that accepts electrons or donates protons; usually has a sour, sharp, or biting taste.

alkali A soluble salt obtained from the ashes of plants.

aquifer An underground bed or layer of water.

atom The smallest part of an element.

base A water-soluble and bitter-tasting compound.

chemical reaction A change in which one kind of matter is turned into another kind of matter.

electrolysis A process that produces chemical changes by the passage of an electric current.

electron A negatively charged particle found outside the nucleus of an atom.

fibrous Having or resembling fiber or stringy tissue.

ion A particle that is positively or negatively charged; an atom that has lost or gained one or more electrons.

isotope An atom of a chemical element with the same atomic number and nearly identical chemical behavior but with a different atomic weight and different physical properties.

matter Material substance that occupies space.

molecule The smallest bit of matter before it gets broken down into its basic parts, or atoms.

neutron A particle within the nucleus of an atom that contains no charge; found in the nucleus of all elements except hydrogen.

nucleus The positively charged center portion of an atom.

proton A positively charged particle within the nucleus of an atom. The number of protons and electrons are almost always equal in an atom.

For More Information

American Chemical Society
1155 Sixteenth Street NW
Washington, DC 20036
e-mail: help@acs.org
Web site: http://www.acs.org

National Geographic Society
1145 Seventeenth Street NW
Washington, DC 20036
Web site: http://www.nationalgeographic.com/kids

The Smithsonian Institution
Smithsonian Center for Education and Museum Studies
P.O. Box 37012
A&I 1163, MRC 402
Washington, DC 20013
e-mail: educate@si.edu
Web site: http://www.smithsonian.kids.us

Web Sites

Due to the changing nature of Internet links, the Rosen Publishing Group, Inc., has developed an online list of Web sites related to the subject of this book. This site is updated regularly. Please use this link to access the list:

http://www.rosenlinks.com/uept/sodi

For Further Reading

Atkins, P. W. *The Periodic Kingdom: A Journey into the Land of the Chemical Elements.* New York: Basic Books, 1997.

Karukstis, Kerry K., and Gerald Van Hecke. *Chemistry Connections: The Chemical Basis of Everyday Phenomena.* New York: Academic Press, 2003.

Nelson, Robin. *From Sea to Salt.* Minneapolis: Lerner Publications Company, 2003.

Newmark, Ann. *Chemistry.* New York: DK Publishing, 1999.

Oxlade, Chris. *Elements & Compounds.* Portsmouth, NH: Heinemann Library, 2002.

Bibliography

Emsley, John. *Nature's Building Blocks: An A-Z Guide to the Elements.* New York: Oxford University Press, 2002.

Heiserman, David L. *Exploring Chemical Elements and Their Compounds.* New York: McGraw-Hill, 1991.

Kurlansky, Mark. *Salt: A World History.* New York: Walker and Co., 2002.

Lemay, H. Eugene, Jr., et al. *Chemistry: Connections to Our Changing World.* Englewood Cliffs, NJ: Prentice Hall, 2002.

Stwertka, Albert. *A Guide to the Elements.* New York: Oxford University Press Children's Books, 1999.

About the Author

Journalist and freelance editor Michele Thomas has covered health and nutrition for *Muscle Media* magazine and was the managing editor of Metro Newspaper Service. She has also worked on science programs for Newbridge Educational Publishing and Macmillan/McGraw-Hill. She lives in her native Brooklyn, New York, with Stitches the cat.

Photo Credits

Cover, pp. 1, 11, 13, 19, 22, 24, 31, 38, 42–43 by Tahara Hasan; pp. 5, 16 © Hulton/Archive/Getty Images; p. 6 © Bettmann/Corbis; p. 8 © The Royal Institution, London, UK / Bridgeman Art Library; pp. 9, 14, 35 by Maura McConnell; p. 18 © Scott Camazine/Photo Researchers, Inc.; p. 26 © Scott T. Smith/Corbis; p. 28 © Owen Franken/Corbis; p. 33 © Biophoto Associates/Photo Researchers, Inc.; p. 34 © Otto Rogge/Corbis; p. 40 © Roger Viollet/Getty Images; p. 41 © J. Bavosi/Photo Researchers, Inc.

Special thanks to Rosemarie Alken and the Westtown School, in Westtown, Pennsylvania.

Designer: Tahara Hasan; Editor: Charles Hofer